Take-Along Guide

Flamingos, Loons and Pelicans

by Mel Boring

illustrations by Andrew Recher

NORTHWORD
Minnetonka, Minnesota

DEDICATION

To Dr. Gwen,
who helped me turn on lights in my life
that are still burning brightly —M.B.

ACKNOWLEDGMENTS

The author would like to thank:

Jim Doidge, Naturalist at the Mitchell County Conservation Center
near Osage, Iowa, who heads its Trumpeter Swan Restoration Project;
and The University of Iowa Libraries, especially the Biology Library
and the Main Library, whose staffs are always helpful and patient.

Text © 2006 by Mel Boring

NorthWord

Books for Young Readers
11571 K-Tel Drive
Minnetonka, MN 55343
www.tnkidsbooks.com

Edited by Kristen McCurry
Designed by Lois A. Rainwater
Illustrated by Andrew Recher
Craft consultant: Heidi Kroll
Roger Tory Peterson quote from "Star Billing," by Les Line,
National Wildlife, April/May 1999, Vol. 347, Issue 3.

Library of Congress Cataloging-in-Publication Data

Boring, Mel.
Flamingos, loons and pelicans / by Mel Boring ; illustrations by Andrew Recher.
p. cm. -- (Take-along guide)
ISBN 1-55971-942-7 (hardcover) -- ISBN 1-55971-943-5 (pbk.)
1. Flamingos--Juvenile literature. 2. Loons--Juvenile literature.
3. Pelicans--Juvenile literature. I. Recher, Andrew, ill. II. Title. III. Series.

QL696.C56B67 2006
598.176--dc22   2005018745

Printed in Malaysia
10 9 8 7 6 5 4 3 2 1

CONTENTS

Flamingos, Loons and Pelicans

INTRODUCTION

All birds drink water, and many take baths in it. But about 40 percent of birds need to stay in or near water, and they are called *water birds*. Living by a body of water is as much a part of a water bird's life as its wings or its nest.

Water birds might live next to a small stream, as belted kingfishers do, or on a tiny pond, like mallards. Or they might live along a mighty ocean, like some herring gulls. Other water birds' homes may be on or next to other bodies of water, such as swamps or rivers. You probably have some water birds living near you.

Some water birds swim or wade in the water, and some just nest near it. *Waterfowl* is the word for a water bird that swims. Some, such as common loons, swim with great skill. Other water birds swim a little, but not all water birds swim. Some are just waders, like the long-legged greater flamingo.

The unique sounds water birds make will help you recognize them.

A few water birds, such as the American white pelican and wood stork, make very little sound, and are often silent. Most make some noise, but one of these water birds, the American bittern, has perhaps the most unusual call of any bird in the world. It sounds like a factory machine!

Water birds have special feathers, too. Their feathers have to give them complete waterproofing, because if water gets through their feathers and soaks their bodies, some water birds could freeze to death. One water bird has some most unusual feathers called "powder-downs." You will find out more about these when you read about the great blue heron.

Use the scrapbook pages in the back to draw pictures or make lists of the water birds you see. And you can use the ruler on the back cover to help with the fun activities in this book. Turn the page, and enter the wide world of water birds!

MALLARD

WHAT IS THIS BIRD LIKE?

The mallard is a world-famous duck. It lives in North and Central America, Europe, Asia, and Africa. Nearly everyone recognizes the male mallard, from glossy green head and yellow bill, to rust-colored chest, to yellow legs and feet.

Female mallards wear more plain colors. They are light and dark brown, with brown-spotted underside, white throat, and dark brown cap.

Mallards eat with their heads underwater and bottoms straight up. This is called "dabbling," and mallards dabble in shallow water less than 2 feet (0.6 m) deep. So they are sometimes called "pond ducks," or "puddle ducks." Newborn ducklings learn to swim as soon as their feathers dry.

INTERESTING FACTS

The mallard is the ancestor of almost all the ducks you see in any barnyard. It is the "grandducky" of most white ducks with yellow beaks, legs, and feet.

WHAT MAKES IT SPECIAL?

Mallards are experts at waddling. And they don't need a running start to fly off land or water. They leap right to flight, taking off almost straight up. Mallards are fast fliers, reaching speeds up to 60 miles per hour (97 kph). Because mallards live in so many places, they eat all different kinds of foods. From grains to flowers to seeds to tree leaves to fish and frogs—a huge menu!

WHAT DOES IT SOUND LIKE?

The song of male and female mallards is one of simple quacks. The female's song is loud, clear quacks, like: *quack-quack-quack, quack, quack-quack*. The male sings higher, squawkier notes: *kwek-kwek-kwek*.

Here's a sure way to recognize male mallards: they always have curly tails. Not like a twisty pig tail, but with two curled-up black feathers at their tail end. In fact, one of the mallard's other names is "curly-tail."

COMMON LOON

WHAT IS THIS BIRD LIKE?

The common loon has bright feathering, with a dark green-black-purple head, white-checkered back with black bars, white-spotted black wings, and white underside.

The loon is a big bird with small wings. From beak to tail, a common loon can measure 1 yard (0.9 m). Yet the loon has narrow, pointed wings, with the least wing surface for its weight of any flying bird. So it has take-off problems.

Loons can only take off from water. With their short stubby legs and huge webbed feet they are stumblebums on land. When they fly up off the water, they need a long "runway," 25 yards to 1/2 mile (23 m–0.8 km), to get airborne.

WHAT DOES IT SOUND LIKE?

The loon's calls sound like crazy laughter. Its yodel is one of its weirdest. It starts low, then rises and stays high: *yodel-ha-oo-oo*. Males use it to defend their territory, especially when they have little loon chicks. It's their warning to back off.

"Crazy as a loon" is a saying people use. But it's only because of the loon's crazy-laugh call. A loon is just as sensible as any other bird.

WHAT MAKES IT SPECIAL?

Loons' huge feet and heavy bodies make them expert divers. A loon is one of few birds with solid bones—no air pockets inside. So it can sink far below the surface to find food. Loons have been known to dive 600 feet (183 m)—as far down as a 60-story building goes up!

Loons can stay underwater for as long as 5 minutes and swim 300 to 400 yards (274–366 m) to escape enemies. They have sleek bodies like submarines, driven by their big feet. Usually, loon dives last 30 to 45 seconds.

INTERESTING FACTS

Loons are some of our most primitive birds. Loon bones have been found in Ice Age glacial deposits from about 2 million years ago.

CANADA GOOSE

WHAT IS THIS BIRD LIKE?

"Honker" is the favorite name for this waterfowl. In the Canada goose's range—from the Arctic, to Canada, to most of the United States—they are the big birds you see and hear overhead in spring and fall, migrating north or south. They often fly in perfect Vs. They're called Canada geese because once most of these birds were born in Canada.

WHAT MAKES IT SPECIAL?

Canada geese graze on grasses growing in wetlands. When a flock of honkers is eating, there is always a guard goose to honk at danger. The guard watches especially closely if there are goslings.

A hundred years ago, Canadas were overhunted until people thought they had become extinct. But in the 1960s a flock was discovered near Rochester, Minnesota.

Wildlife managers began to capture the geese and breed them so they could restore them to their original habitat. After being penned in, however, some Canada geese forgot about migration and just stayed in one place.

INTERESTING FACTS

The wings of the Canada goose are powerful enough to beat off attacks from enemies like foxes, and sometimes people.

The plan to restore the Canada geese population may have been too successful because in some places there were now too many geese. By the year 2000 there were 4 to 5 million geese in the United States, and some people felt they were becoming pests on lawns and golf courses. Stepping on goose droppings was yucky. Some communities relocated their geese to far-away places, or even killed them. First they were brought back; then they were being destroyed.

WHAT DOES IT SOUND LIKE?

Honk-a-lonk is the sound coming from the sky as Canada geese fly by. Listen for the Canada's honk overhead in the spring. It's a sign that a thaw is on the way, because honkers time their migration to arrive when the ice in their breeding grounds is about to melt.

ROSEATE SPOONBILL

WHAT IS THIS BIRD LIKE?

This water bird is mostly rose-pink, and its beak is shaped like a spoon. That's how the roseate [ROW-zee-it] spoonbill gets its name. This water bird is a brilliant rainbow, from white to pink to red to yellow to orange to green to blue to brown to gray to black.

Spoonbill chicks are not born rosy, but mostly white. They are fed from their parents' bill "spoons." They poke their beaks way down inside and eat heartily the food brought up for them. The chicks soon develop some pink coloring, mixed in with their white and gray feathers.

This red-eyed firebird eats by "sweep-feeding," walking about waving its wide bill in a half-circle under the water. It catches killifish, minnows, water bugs, frogs, and shrimp that swim between its jaws.

INTERESTING FACTS

The spoonbill usually feeds in water up to its knees with its bill in the water. It is able to breathe while doing this because its nostrils are very high up on its bill.

WHAT MAKES IT SPECIAL?

It's the bill of the roseate spoonbill that makes it special; no other American bird has one like it. Not only is its bill wide like a spoon, but it also makes an excellent sifter for straining tiny food morsels out of water and mud.

WHAT DOES IT SOUND LIKE?

The call of this "Rosy Spoonbill" is low, a kind of grunted *huh-huh-huh-huh*, always at the same tone and loudness. Sometimes it turns into a higher dry rasp that is swifter: *rek-ek-ek-ek-ek-ek*. The low croaking notes sound like spoonbills are chatting with each other.

The world-famous bird expert Roger Tory Peterson called roseate spoonbills "one of the most breathtaking of the world's weird birds."

GREATER FLAMINGO

WHAT IS THIS BIRD LIKE?

This flamingo is the brightest pink bird in the world. It is all pink, except for its yellow eyes, black beak tip, and black flight feathers, which are the rows of feathers under the wings. Flamingos are mostly neck and legs, about 5 feet (1.5 m) tall, yet weigh only about 5 pounds (2.3 kg).

The flamingos' stilty legs are about half their body. They have longer legs for their body size than any other bird. Their wingspan is as wide as they are tall.

WHAT MAKES IT SPECIAL?

A flamingo is an "upside-down filter-feeder." Its bill is bent down at the middle. So when it sticks its bill in the water to feed, the bill goes back between its legs, upside down, and works like a cup. Then the top of the bill is on the bottom, and scoops up mucky water with tiny creatures, such as algae and small fish.

INTERESTING FACTS

Flamingo nests look like anthills rising up out of the muddy shores they are built on. The birds scoop up mud for the nests with their bills, then pat it with their wide webbed feet, forming a cone cut off at the top.

Flamingos pump their tongue to filter the water through slits in their billtops. Then they swallow the rich "soup" that's left.

Most flamingos are born outside the United States, along the shores of Caribbean islands. Years ago, there were no flamingos born in the U.S. But then some came to live at the horserace track in Hialeah Park near Miami, Florida. The park has a lake with four islands, and is now home to about 900 flamingos.

WHAT DOES IT SOUND LIKE?

The song of the flamingos is a honk that sounds much like barnyard geese, only deeper. It's a low *onk* and *ohrn*. When flamingo flocks are milling about a beach, they gabble among themselves.

HOW DO THEY DO THAT?

SPECIAL FEATURES OF WATER BIRDS

If you lived in the water, you would need a special way to find your food. Two birds have very unusual beaks, sometimes called bills, to help catch their favorites.

How do spoonbills find food? The spoonbill has a special beak shaped like two spoons. As the spoonbill walks through the water, its long toes stir up minnows, water bugs, frogs, and shrimp. This brings the food closer to the surface so the bird can skim it off the top.

WHAT YOU NEED TO BE A SPOONBILL:

- 2 plastic spoons
- pan of muddy water with several marbles and small pebbles

Sweep the spoons back and forth to stir up the "creatures" in your pan. With your spoons, try to scoop up the muddy water to see what you can catch.

How do flamingos find food? Flamingos hunt for shrimp and small snails that live near the bottom of water. The top half of the flamingo's beak is bent and has openings for water to filter out.

The flamingo bends its head down and sweeps its beak upside down through the water. The slotted part of the beak scoops up what it can and filters out the water. Then the bird eats the remaining "soup," full of delicious seafood!

WHAT YOU NEED TO BE A FLAMINGO:

- slotted serving spoon
- wooden spoon
- pan of water with some dried beans or small pebbles

Get your flamingo beak ready by holding the slotted spoon on top and the wooden spoon on the bottom. Stand above the pan of water, then put your head upside down between your legs, like a football player about to hike the ball. Scoop up a spoonful from the pan, wait for the water to drain out, and then count your catch!

If you swam in the water all the time, you would need special feet.

How do ducks swim? Birds that swim usually have webbed feet. The skin that connects their toes helps ducks to get through the water better and more quickly, especially in case of danger. If you have ever worn flippers on your feet when you swim, you already know how ducks move!

WHAT YOU NEED TO BE A DUCK:

- deep pan or sink of water (You can try this one in the bathtub or in the pool!)
- small cover from a plastic container

Put your hand into the water and pull your open fingers through it. Notice how the water flows right between your fingers because your fingers are thin and have little resistance. Now hold the plastic cover against your fingers with your thumb to create a "webbed" hand, and run it through the water again. Can you feel the difference? This is how ducks push against the water to swim quickly. Try this next time you go swimming, and see how much faster you can go!

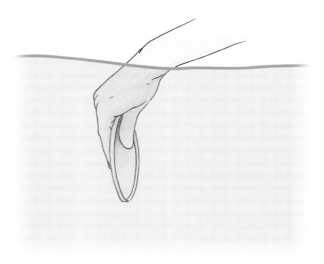

TRUMPETER SWAN

WHAT IS THIS BIRD LIKE?

Trumpeter swans are the largest water birds in North America. They grow to an average 65 inches (165 cm) long—as long as most mountain bikes. Their wingspan can be 8 1/2 feet (2.6 m). Adults weigh 25 to 35 pounds (11–16 kg).

Trumpeter swans are white all over, with yellowish patches. And they look like they're wearing black half-masks. Their black bills have peaks reaching to their eyes.

The trumpeter swan is another food "dabbler." Plunging its head and long neck underwater, it goes "bottoms-up." It rips up water plants from the bottom. Swans' favorite food is duckweed.

WHAT MAKES IT SPECIAL?

In the early 1900s, many people thought trumpeter swans were nearly extinct. Traders were snatching their feathers to sell for hat-making and their skins for powder puffs. By 1932, only 69 trumpeters could be found in the United States. Starting in 1938, swan babies, or cygnets, were taken to wildlife refuges for protection.

Beginning in 1966, some states started programs to bring the swans back to their home habitat. Minnesota was first, followed by Wisconsin, Michigan, South Dakota, Iowa, Missouri, and Nebraska. Today there are at least 6,000 trumpeters, and maybe as many as 13,000. They live 20 to 30 years.

WHAT DOES IT SOUND LIKE?

Why are they called trumpeters? Because of their raspy bugle honk. It sounds like *ko-ho*, with long Os, like a person playing the trumpet for the first time. They sound their call while swimming or flying. Cygnets honk and fly at only 3 months old.

If you think trumpeter swans are smiling at you, maybe it's because of the pink "smile line" along their lower beak. Smile back— and honk if you love trumpeter swans!

HERRING GULL

WHAT IS THIS BIRD LIKE?

When we hear "sea gull," we usually picture this herring gull, our most widespread gull. Herrings come in many sizes, shapes, and colors. Any two of them can look as different as the sun and moon. The differences are mostly because of age.

For their first winter, herring gulls are brown, mottled with darker brown, black, gray, and white feathers, and they have a black bill. In their first spring, they molt (shed old feathers) and their new feathers are lighter colored. Their bills turn pinkish.

It takes 3 years for herrings to get full adult coloring. As they molt each spring and fall, they get closer. Adults have a white neck and underparts, black wing tips with white spots, and pink legs. Their silver-gray back looks like a vest.

WHAT MAKES IT SPECIAL?

Herring chicks get "push-button meals." Adults have a bright red spot on their bills. When babies peck at the spot, parents bring up digested food to put in their chicks' beaks.

Herring gulls prefer fish and other animal food when they can get it, but will eat nearly anything. They are excellent scavengers, and their favorite restaurants may be fast food dumpsters with burgers and fries!

Herring gulls help us by cleaning up dead fish and eatable garbage along our beaches. They also lead fishing boats to schools of herring fish, which this bird's name came from. Herrings also love shellfish, and are experts at cracking them. They catch them, then fly up high and drop them on rocks below.

WHAT DOES IT SOUND LIKE?

Herring gulls are noisy, and their rowdy shouts are part of the charm of seaside towns along our Atlantic Coast. It just wouldn't seem like a New England village without the herring gull's *kaaw, kaaw, kaaw!*

INTERESTING FACTS

Herring gulls live long lives. One was banded as a chick in Denmark in 1925, and found again in 1953, 28 years later. All their long lives, they are very social birds, hunting, resting, scavenging, and quarreling together.

21

SANDHILL CRANE

WHAT IS THIS BIRD LIKE?

The strut of the sandhill crane looks surprisingly close to a person's upright walk. This bird stands about 4 feet (1.2 m) tall and walks nearly straight-up. Sandhills are gray, with white cheeks, chin, and throat, and their naked, bright red forehead sets them apart from other birds. Their outstretched wings can span 6 1/2 feet (2 m). Sandhill cranes have a fluff of secondary feathers hanging down like a tail.

With a few long running strides, sandhill cranes fly off. Migrating cranes travel as high as 2 miles (3.2 km) up in a strong V-shape or one even beak-to-tail line. During their spring and fall migrations between Siberia and as far south as Cuba, thousands of them stop over at places such as southeast Nebraska— sometimes as many as 100,000 cranes. It's a sight people from all over the world come to see.

INTERESTING FACTS

Corn from the shock is a favorite meal of sandhills. They also eat insects, frogs, lizards, snakes, and mice. They poke into soft ground with their strong bills for roots and grubs, too.

WHAT MAKES IT SPECIAL?

Sandhill cranes put on elegant mating dance displays. They walk tensely around each other with quick steps and wings half-spread. They leap into the air—as high as 6 to 8 feet (1.8–2.4 m)—with feet flung forward. They pick up pieces of grass in their bills, throw them upward, and stab at them as they fall. This swinging dance is usually done in breeding season, but also at other times, seemingly just to "let off steam."

WHAT DOES IT SOUND LIKE?

Cranes have very special windpipes, twisting inside them like trumpet coils. This gives sandhills one of the most resounding calls of any bird. It's a blaring, trumpety note: *gur-roo, gar-oo-oo-oo,* or *garoo-oo-a-a-a-a.* A loud, deep, rolling hornblast that can be heard a mile (1.6 km) away.

BELTED KINGFISHER

that make their bodies seem small by comparison. Kingfishers are bigger than blue jays—13 inches (33 cm) long.

Their underparts are white, and a chin-strap looks like it's holding a blue-gray cape on their backs. The female also wears a rust-colored belt. She gives them their name, "belted" kingfisher. Unlike most birds, female kingfishers are more colorful than males.

An old legend says the kingfisher was once a colorless bird, but got its colors by flying straight west into the setting sun. The sun scorched the female's belly red, while both kingfishers' backs reflected the gray-blue of the evening sky behind them.

WHAT IS THIS BIRD LIKE?

The belted kingfisher lives anywhere in Canada and the United States where there is any kind of water. It has been spotted at beaver ponds in Utah, as well as on beams beneath an East River bridge in New York City.

Belted kingfishers are chunky birds with short necks and tails, but huge heads and beaks. They appear smaller than they are because they have unusually large heads

WHAT MAKES IT SPECIAL?

The belted kingfisher is a wily fisherbird. It perches on a bare branch over the water, and watches. When it spies a fish, it plunges down headfirst, grabs it with its sharp beak, and carries it back up to eat. Kingfishers can also hover 20, even 50 feet (6–15 m) above the water until a fish comes near the surface. Then they dive, and beak-spear it.

WHAT DOES IT SOUND LIKE?

Kingfishers have loud calls, but they are not musical. Screeching on the ground or while flying, their call is a quick string of noises like a clackety New Year's Eve noisemaker—*tck-tck-tck-tck-tck!*

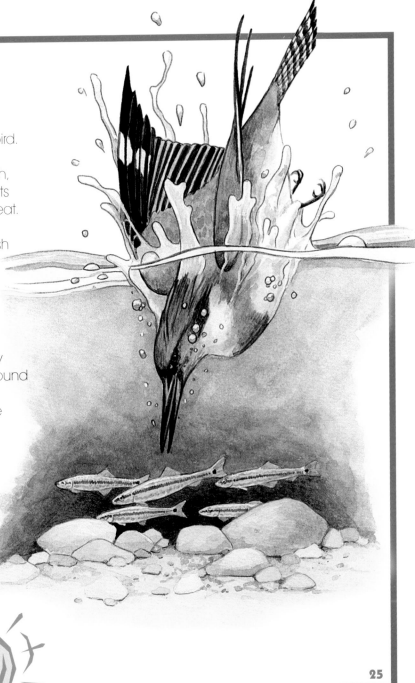

INTERESTING FACTS

The kingfisher couple builds their nest by digging a tunnel sideways into the dry sand or clay of stream-banks. These burrows sometimes slant upward, and are 3 to 15 feet (0.9–4.6 m) long, ending in a round hollow for the nest.

AMERICAN WHITE PELICAN

WHAT IS THIS BIRD LIKE?

A wonderful bird is the pelican,
His mouth can hold more than his belly can.
He can hold in his beak,
enough food for a week!...

So goes a rhyme by Dixon Lanier Merritt about this water bird with the huge beak. A pelican's bill looks like many other birds', but the lower part blows up like a balloon.

The American white pelican is one of America's largest birds, growing nearly 6 feet (1.8 m) long with a wingspan up to 10 feet (3 m). They're so big that they have problems getting airborne. They pitter-patter along clumsily, trying to gain enough speed to fly.

Pelicans stay together, eating or resting. They behave like soldiers—what one does, everyone does. They all face the same way when sitting. They fly like airplanes in formation, evenly spaced, wings beating together.

INTERESTING FACTS

But can a pelican's beak really hold enough food for a week? Their beak holds about 3 gallons (11.4 l), and the pelican needs about that much food every day. So a pelican's beak-full of food is not enough for a week!

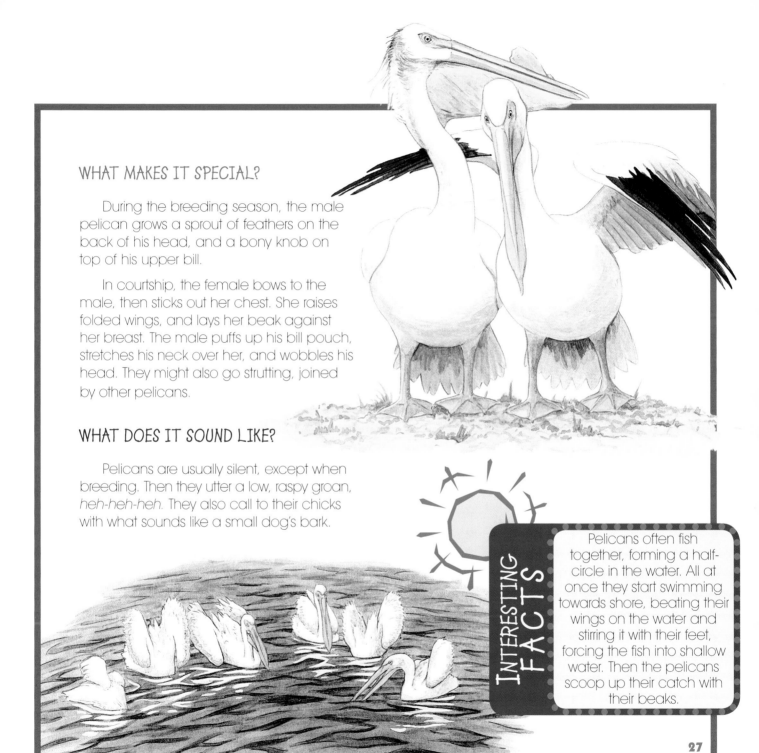

WHAT MAKES IT SPECIAL?

During the breeding season, the male pelican grows a sprout of feathers on the back of his head, and a bony knob on top of his upper bill.

In courtship, the female bows to the male, then sticks out her chest. She raises folded wings, and lays her beak against her breast. The male puffs up his bill pouch, stretches his neck over her, and wobbles his head. They might also go strutting, joined by other pelicans.

WHAT DOES IT SOUND LIKE?

Pelicans are usually silent, except when breeding. Then they utter a low, raspy groan, *heh-heh-heh*. They also call to their chicks with what sounds like a small dog's bark.

INTERESTING FACTS

Pelicans often fish together, forming a half-circle in the water. All at once they start swimming towards shore, beating their wings on the water and stirring it with their feet, forcing the fish into shallow water. Then the pelicans scoop up their catch with their beaks.

MAKE YOUR OWN BIRD TRACKS

Even if you don't have water birds in your neighborhood, you can make their footprints! Plan to make at least two different bird prints. Try the webbed foot of the flamingo or pelican, and choose one of the long-toed wading or perching birds, such as the kingfisher or spoonbill. Make one batch of plaster for each foot. You have to work quickly before it sets.

YOU WILL NEED:

- plaster of Paris powder
- water
- plastic bowl or disposable container
- plastic spoon
- plastic measuring cup
- pie pan, box, or bottom cut from milk carton (with sides about 1 inch [2.5 cm] deep)
- straight sticks or twigs
- plastic wrap

Following are "toe" sizes of each suggested bird. You may need to make smaller versions of these feet to fit in your dish.

KINGFISHER
1.5 inches (3.8 cm)

SPOONBILL
5 inches (12.7 cm)

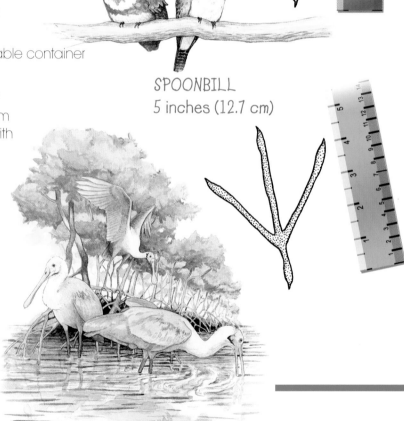

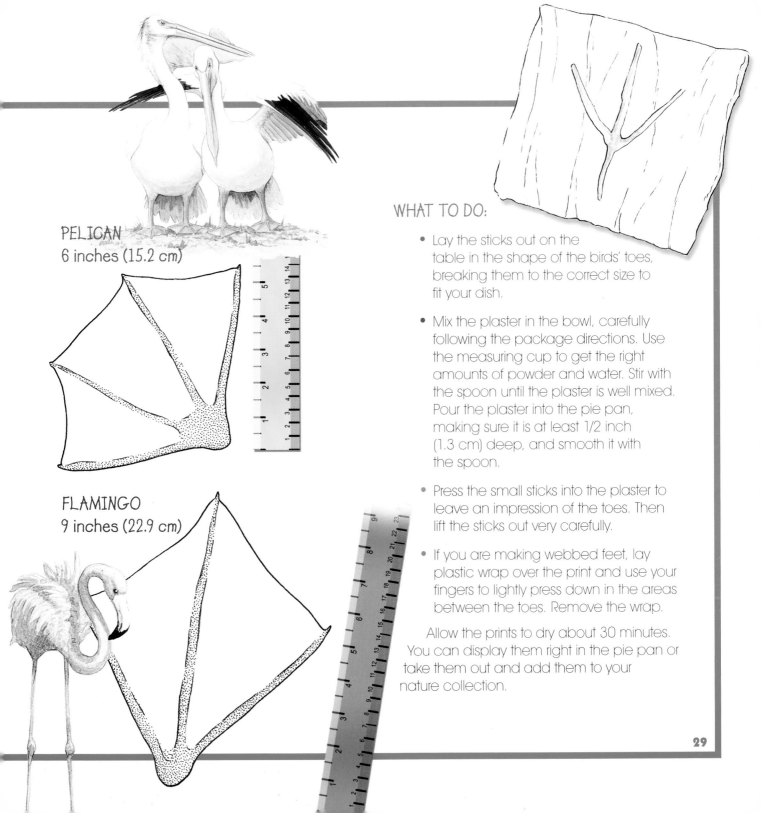

PELICAN
6 inches (15.2 cm)

FLAMINGO
9 inches (22.9 cm)

WHAT TO DO:

- Lay the sticks out on the table in the shape of the birds' toes, breaking them to the correct size to fit your dish.

- Mix the plaster in the bowl, carefully following the package directions. Use the measuring cup to get the right amounts of powder and water. Stir with the spoon until the plaster is well mixed. Pour the plaster into the pie pan, making sure it is at least 1/2 inch (1.3 cm) deep, and smooth it with the spoon.

- Press the small sticks into the plaster to leave an impression of the toes. Then lift the sticks out very carefully.

- If you are making webbed feet, lay plastic wrap over the print and use your fingers to lightly press down in the areas between the toes. Remove the wrap.

Allow the prints to dry about 30 minutes. You can display them right in the pie pan or take them out and add them to your nature collection.

29

SNOWY EGRET

WHAT IS THIS BIRD LIKE?

You've probably seen the snowy egret on stamps issued by the U.S. Postal Service in 2003. This water bird is without question the loveliest of all the heron family. You can spot this egret by its black legs with bright yellow feet, or "golden slippers."

The snowy is just about 2 feet long (0.6 m), all white, weighing less than 1 pound (0.5 kg). During breeding season it grows 50 fancy feathers down its back, as well as a chest feather crest. Curvy head plumes make it look like it's wearing a fancy hat.

Snowy egrets were hunted to make fancy hats for people a hundred years ago. It took 4 birds to get just an ounce (28 g) of their delicate, snow-white feathers. They were in such demand that hunters hunted egrets to near extinction. Nearly 200,000 egrets were killed between 1885 and 1910.

Through the Migratory Bird Treaty Act of Congress in 1918, snowy egrets and other birds were saved from being wiped out. Since then, egrets have been enlarging their range northward in the United States.

WHAT MAKES IT SPECIAL?

Dainty and nimble, snowy egrets "feed on the run." They race about in shallow water, chasing fish and shrimp. They whip up the water with their feet and scurry back and forth, chasing fish in a food frenzy. Then they spear them with their javelin-like bill. These waders also snatch up fish while flying low over water.

WHAT DOES IT SOUND LIKE?

The "little snowy" is usually silent, but not when it utters its *AWWWK!* of a squawk! It makes you feel as if you're scraping your fingernails down a chalkboard.

INTERESTING FACTS

When the mother and father egrets relieve each other on the nest, they display their fancy feathers to each other, as if out of politeness. When the baby snowies hatch, the parents make a similar feathery display to the young birds as they bring them food.

GREAT BLUE HERON

WHAT IS THIS BIRD LIKE?

Great blue herons are really mostly gray-blue. Their white neck front has black streaks, and a showy plume tops their heads. You would notice great blues in bird gatherings because of their giant size. About 4 feet (1.2 m) tall, they can grow to 52 inches (1.3 m) long from beak to tail, and weigh about 5 1/2 pounds (2.5 kg). They are the largest and most royal-looking herons of all.

Like some other water birds, herons have "powder-downs," unusual kinds of feathers that never fall out. They grow at the bottoms of the regular feathers and their fuzzy tops turn into powder, which the herons pluck off and use to preen their other feathers. Herons use this powder to "dry clean" grease and slime out of their feathers.

WHAT MAKES IT SPECIAL?

The great blue's hunting methods are special. It hunts two ways. First, great blues "still-fish," standing rock-still until fish swim up close. Then they shoot out their long necks with narrow, dagger-like bills to grab them. Or they might "still-hunt," slowly and stealthily tracking fish down.

The great blue can also land on the water just long enough to snatch a fish, then rise back into the air and fly easily away. That is an amazing feat for a bird that is a "wader," but not a good swimmer.

WHAT DOES IT SOUND LIKE?

The great blue's call is a low-note croak. Sometimes in flight, it gives out a very gruff, trumpet-like *fraaahnk*, or *braak*. Their call notes are harsh and squawky. "Big cranky" is a good nickname for this rather noisy bird, which calls out often while flying.

INTERESTING FACTS

Great blue herons usually build big-stick nests in trees, 50 to 100 feet (15–31 m) above the ground.

AMERICAN BITTERN

recognize it is the long black streak on each cheek. If you came close, it might fly up and away with remarkably rapid wing beats.

WHAT MAKES IT SPECIAL?

But the bittern doesn't usually fly away. Instead, it hides by "freezing" on the spot. With feathers pressed close against its body, the bittern stands up straight, pointing its bill upward. Playing " freeze tag," its shape is sleek and its stripes look like weeds, so it blends right into its marsh home.

WHAT DOES IT SOUND LIKE?

The American bittern may have the strangest call in the whole world of birds. When birdwatchers first heard the bittern's "thunder-pumping," they thought it must be coming from some kind of machine. Its deep, throaty PUMP-ER-LUNK didn't sound like any living creature.

The bittern's call can be heard for 1/4 to 1/2 mile (0.4–0.8 km), sounding like an old-fashioned hand water pump, with a

WHAT IS THIS BIRD LIKE?

The American bittern is more easily heard than seen, even though it grows as long as 28 inches (71.1 cm) with a wingspan of 42 inches (1 m). It is a totally secret bird that never flocks with other bitterns. This water bird spends most of its life hiding.

An American bittern's feathering is colored with rich browns and tans, plus a mottle of stripes and spots. The best way to

noisy suction of air taken in, followed by a pumping *thunk*. The bittern swallows air, then kind of belches out its call. Its three-part shout is repeated five or six times, like pounding a stake into the mud with a sledgehammer.

In fact, its mysterious call earned the American bittern the name "stake driver." It sounds more like a construction site than a live bird's call.

INTERESTING FACTS

American bitterns eat snakes, mice, fish, or insects from the marshes they live in—but they like frogs the best.

SPOTTED SANDPIPER

the spotted sandpiper stand out. The "spottie's" spots disappear in winter, however.

Most spotted sandpiper chicks are raised by their father, who becomes a "househusband" in charge of everything from the incubation of the eggs to flying lessons.

Spotted sandpipers eat food from the water, including insects, shrimp, crabs, and small fish. They can "dive for dinner," going totally underwater to chase a good meal.

WHAT IS THIS BIRD LIKE?

The spotted sandpiper is gray-brown on top, and only about 8 inches (20.3 cm) long. And, unusually for birds, the female is larger than the male. The easiest way to spot this water bird is to look for its dark brown and black spots on a white underside. These spots and the white line across each eye make

INTERESTING FACTS

The spotted sandpiper's nest is a hole scraped in the ground, lined with moss, grass, feathers, and weeds. It is sometimes raised a little ways up off the ground.

WHAT MAKES IT SPECIAL?

The spotted sandpiper's head is constantly bopping up and down, and so is its tail. This teetering makes it look as if sandpipers were listening to rock music. You can find these birds in the United States from coast to coast, anywhere there's water. From steep creek banks to ocean shores, spotties are everywhere.

These are wading birds, and they seem to love skittering among pebbles on the beach. There you can see them, dipping their tails up and down, and rushing to the water with wings held stiffly, half-unfolded.

WHAT DOES IT SOUND LIKE?

If the spotted sandpiper is listening to rock music, its call provides the beat: *peet-weet, peet-weet* and sometimes *weet-weet*. They are sometimes called "peet-weets" because of this call, or "tip-ups" because of waggling their bottoms up and down. They are also called "teeter-peeps." What name do you like best for them?

WOOD STORK

WHAT IS THIS BIRD LIKE?

The wood stork is strong-winged. It flies for a while flapping its wings, then it glides. You can recognize wood storks in the sky by the arrow-straight line from outstretched beak to their long legs straight out behind.

On the ground, you can see that wood storks are bald-headed. They are white with black flight feathers. They're different from any other big white bird because of these black wing edges and black tail. And they have pink feet.

WHAT MAKES IT SPECIAL?

Wood storks don't find their food with their eyes, as other birds do. The swamps they fish in are usually muddy and weedy, so they can't see the topminnows and sunfish they like. Instead, they use their sense of touch. Walking slowly through shallow water with heads down, they sweep their open beak back and forth beneath the water, kind of like a weed wacker.

At the same time, they stir up the water ahead with one claw, churning up water creatures. When anything touches a wood stork's beak, it snaps shut automatically in 1/40 of a second! This way it traps tadpoles, fish, snakes, insects, and other critters.

Female and male wood storks spread their wings like umbrellas over their nestlings to protect them from high heat and heavy rain that threaten their chicks' lives.

WHAT DOES IT SOUND LIKE?

Adult wood storks have almost no voice but sometimes express themselves by clacking their bills. At the nestside they make snorty little barks to their young, *unc-unc-unc*. But a nesting colony full of young chicks makes a clamor of grunts, squeals, and other calls that can be heard from far away.

Maybe it was this gabble of sounds that earned the wood stork the nickname "Colorado turkey."

HEAR THE CALLS OF WATER BIRDS

Flamingos, Loons and Pelicans

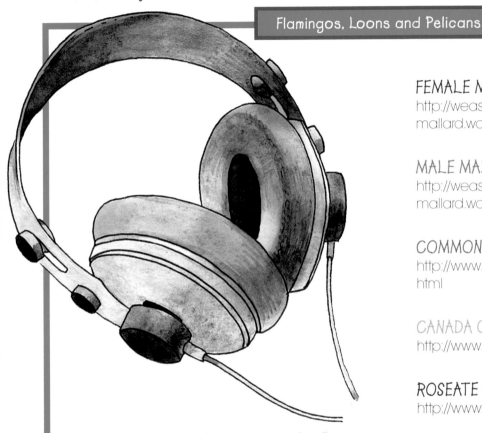

Many water birds have unusual calls, ranging from loud *honks,* to screeching *kaws* to a *peet weet* tweet! You can hear the calls of all the birds in this book by using the Internet sites listed here. At each site you may need to scroll down the page to find an underlined link labeled "sounds," "call," "hear," or "listen."

Which is your favorite? Can you imitate the calls you hear? Next time you're near a pond or lake, listen for the real thing!

FEMALE MALLARD:
http://weaselhead.org/sounds/ns_female_mallard.wav

MALE MALLARD:
http://weaselhead.org/sounds/ns_male_mallard.wav

COMMON LOON:
http://www.ns.ec.gc.ca/wildlife/loons/images.html

CANADA GOOSE:
http://www.gpnc.org/canada.htm

ROSEATE SPOONBILL:
http://www.birding.com/3760rs.asp

GREATER FLAMINGO:
http://www.birds.cornell.edu/programs/AllAboutBirds/audio/Greater_Flamingo.html

TRUMPETER SWAN:
http://www.trumpeterswansociety.org/id.htm

HERRING GULL:
http://www.rspb.org.uk/birds/guide/h/
herringgull/gallery.asp

SANDHILL CRANE (1):
http://www.michiganaudubon.org/
bakersanctuary/crane_calls.html

SANDHILL CRANE (2):
http://www.birds.cornell.edu/programs/
AllAboutBirds/audio/Sandhill_Crane.html

BELTED KINGFISHER:
http://www.birds.cornell.edu/programs/
AllAboutBirds/audio/Belted_Kingfisher.html

AMERICAN WHITE PELICAN:
http://www.enature.com/guides/play_bird_
wm.asp?recnum=BD0174

SNOWY EGRET:
http://www.enature.com/guides/play_bird_wm
.asp?recnum=BD0113&audioPref=wm&submit
1=Set+Format

GREAT BLUE HERON:
http://www.birds.cornell.edu/programs/
AllAboutBirds/audio/Great_Blue_Heron.html

AMERICAN BITTERN:
http://www.enature.com/guides/play_bird_
wm.asp?recnum=BD0108

SPOTTED SANDPIPER:
http://imnh.isu.edu/digitalatlas/bio/birds/gulls/
spsa/spsa_cal.htm

WOOD STORK:
http://www.enature.com/
guides/play_bird_
wm.asp?recnum=BD0247

SAVE OUR WATER BIRDS!

Flamingos, Loons and Pelicans

Many of the birds in this book have faced challenges from environmental pollution and from sharing their world with humans. Following are a few examples of the problems these birds have, as well as some positive changes people are making to protect water birds.

- Airplanes are the worst enemies of flamingos. When one flies near, the birds go into a frenzy and may smash their eggs accidentally. Greater flamingos are a protected species under the Migratory Bird Treaty Act of Congress in 1918.

- Newborn trumpeter swans without any migrating experience, often get tangled in electrical power lines and are electrocuted. That, and people hunting them for sport, are two of the greatest threats to restoring trumpeter swans. Trumpeter swans are also a protected species, and hunting them is not allowed.

- During the "great plume hunt" from 1890 to 1910, spoonbills' fancy feathers were made into fans sold to Florida's winter tourists. Roseate spoonbills disappeared completely from Texas and were almost wiped out in Florida. Today these birds are increasing in Texas, but showing little increase in Florida. Drainage of wetlands for mosquito control and housing development in Florida continue to threaten the feeding grounds of these beautiful birds.

- In the 19th century, thousands of gull eggs were sold in markets as food for people. The populations of these birds nearly disappeared from American coasts before a law was passed almost a hundred years ago, which made it illegal to take gull eggs.

- By the mid-1980s in Florida, because of house building and swamp draining where wood storks had bred, only 250 pairs of storks were left in the Everglades National Park. Other wood storks had migrated to Georgia and South Carolina for breeding, instead. Florida now has plans to restore the

Everglades breeding grounds where wood storks once were plentiful. And thanks to a bill in 1984 that declared wood storks an endangered species, they are now protected, and the populations are increasing again.

Insecticides and other sprays have sometimes poisoned the food and drinking water of birds. But the greatest threat may be oil spills in waters where they make their homes. Because oil is thicker than water, it usually floats on the surface. Water birds—especially swimmers—can become covered in this oil. The oil damages their feathers, allowing water to seep through them and causing the birds to freeze. Oil spills kill a half-million water birds every year. But help is on the way! You can go to the Internet site of the International Bird Rescue Research Center to see how some of these "oiled birds" are being saved: http://www.ibrrc.org.

What else can you do to help? Lots of things!

- You can organize groups of friends and classmates to help clean up garbage from beaches, parks, and other nature areas.

- If you have a pond or stream in your backyard, let the grasses and weeds grow naturally around its edges, instead of mowing or using chemicals near the water. This helps keep the water clean and leaves room for birds and other animals to make nests and hunt for food near their water homes.

- Finally, go bird watching! It's amazing to watch a bird take flight or go for a swim or care for its chicks. But be careful not to disturb birds or their nests. The more you see these fascinating creatures, the better you'll understand their needs and be able to share what you know with others.

SCRAPBOOK

Flamingos, Loons and Pelicans

Flamingos, Loons and Pelicans

Find All Kinds of Stuff . . .

Take-Along Guides

Titles available in the Take-Along Guide series:

NORTHWORD
Minnetonka, Minnesota